Book 1:

Money Marketing Mastery

BY J.J.Jones

&

Book 2:

Money Management Makeover

BY J.J.Jones

Book 1:

Money Marketing Mastery

BY J.J.JONES

Successful Strategies to Mastering Marketing to Make Money!

Table Of Contents

Introduction

I want to thank you and congratulate you for purchasing the book, *"Money Marketing Mastery: Successful Strategies to Mastering Marketing to Make Money!"*

This book contains proven steps and strategies on how to start your marketing career and how to get started to earn more money right now.

Marketing is a lucrative career that you can take if you want a recession-proof and steady of source of income right in the comforts of your home. The internet has provided practically limitless opportunities for marketers to take their careers to the next level without having to spend years of service in marketing companies and other businesses that require traditional marketing services. Today, one of the leading online businesses is internet marketing.

As internet marketing promises the biggest opportunity of making money to today's modern businessmen, this book focuses on the different strategies of mastering marketing to make money starting from scratch up to proper marketing management to gain bigger market share; hence, more money.

As a modern marketer, you will practically promote, sell and refer products and services by other businesses, although you can also market your own products and service but with a different income structure. Once you commit to do marketing, you have to dedicate your time and resources as you will be doing practically everything, from the selection of products and services, doing the marketing research and applying market studies, creating media and marketing materials, identifying markets, interacting with customers and potential markets, to closing a deal and collecting and collating customer feedbacks as part of your market research. A modern marketer is his own team.

In general, you can also apply the tips that will be given here to your own e-commerce business if you manage your own online store or run an actual office-based business with internet marketing arm.

This early, you need to understand that marketing is not as simple as writing an ad or review and posting it in your own blog. Marketing is more complex than that. It is holistic. It needs time and patience because unlike direct selling, it tries to reach larger markets by maximizing various media. If you are up for the challenge, then proceed with the next chapter.

Thanks again for purchasing this book, I hope you enjoy it!

Chapter 1 - Choosing a Promising Product

"Promising" either means the product having a huge market demand with high potential for expansion to other market segments, or a product with high potential to create a demand (like in the case of innovative and unique products). Choosing a product to market is the first strategy towards building a successful career in marketing, whether you choose to venture in affiliate marketing, network marketing, multilevel marketing (MLM), online marketing, attraction marketing, email marketing, direct marketing or social media marketing.

Unfortunately, many marketing novices fail to throw sufficient attention in the products themselves. Rather, they look at their projected earnings, which is not really surprising because earning is their main goal in the first place.

Choosing a good, sellable product is the first important step of starting your marketing career because all your effort will be futile if you will keep on pushing with a product that has no market to begin with. The product and business you are marketing for should meet high standards that make them credible, reputable and reliable. Otherwise, you are just bating yourself for scammers to take advantage.

Investing your time and money on high-paying yet substandard and questionable affiliate programs, networking businesses and MLM structures will cost you more than what you invest; it will cost you your own name, reputation and everything that you work hard for just to get a place in the cutthroat world of the marketing industry where everyone seems to rebuke and malign tough competitors to steal their shares.

Remember that no marketing strategy can save you if the product itself fails to meet the expectations of consumers. On the other hand, a high quality product only needs minimal marketing efforts as its standard sell for itself.

In choosing a product to sell or marketing program to join, consider these six essential factors that determine the probability of your success in the marketing business.

- **Demand.** Also called the gravity of product, there should be an existing market demand, or at least, promising direction, for a type of product before anybody can claim potential for success. This means choosing a relatively new product with not much track record of success as your affiliate product comes with high risk.

  If you think that it is promising but still has no solid market-base just yet, it might be a wiser decision to venture on article marketing, attraction marketing, blogging, direct marketing, SEO marketing or social media marketing instead of affiliate marketing because these types of marketing are more equipped for introductory campaigns than affiliate marketing.

- **High commission.** The point of being a marketer is earning. It is but natural to look for opportunities that pay well. For instance, affiliate marketers normally earn from 4% to 25% of the total selling price of whatever products they are marketing. The commission rates can change depending on demand, average price range, market distribution and product type.

  Affiliate products and services with higher demands normally have lower commission rates because they are easier to market anyway. On the other hand, those that are normally selling at high prices, such as lawn mowers and industrial humidifiers, come with higher commissions because they are harder to market. If a product can be bought from a lot of sources (such as when there are already a lot of affiliate marketers for a particular affiliate program), the commission is also higher because the competition is stiffer.

  Nonetheless, if a company thinks that its affiliate product has high potential for success yet still does not have decent demand, it might give high commission simply to attract more marketers for them.

- **Impressive bonuses and more opportunities.** Affiliate programs usually provide bonuses for excellent performances and sales thresholds, while some offer opportunities to market for bigger commission rates and head a team of their own. These are extra motivators for their affiliates to work harder. Bonuses might include monetary rewards, free products, electronic vouchers, gift certificates, all-expense paid local and foreign trips, free trainings and seminars or leadership positions where they can earn more and be paid with honoraria for managing a team.

  Excellent performances might mean consistent level of referrals, outstanding marketing strategies, innovative marketing and selling techniques or excellent customer feedbacks. For sales threshold, companies usually set non-requirement quotas and commission levels. Hence, dedication and investment of time are necessary if you want to build a solid career in the affiliate marketing industry.

- **Decent return rate.** Return rate means the projected return on investment (ROI) for all the expenditures you might incur, such as websites, paid advertisements, outsourcing requirements, resellers, etc. It can also mean the return of your investment computed for every product you are marketing (your expense per product on periodical basis).

  The actual return rate will be determined by your ability to market and dedication to the work, but companies also have computed return rates that they promise to their affiliates by taking into consideration the maximal or minimal possible sales volumes a marketer can handle per day. This is why you see networking and MLM companies advertise how much their members can earn on a daily or weekly basis.

If a company promises high return rate, the data they used probably comes from the average return rates of their existing affiliates. There are companies that guarantee specific return rates within given period but they are usually the ones that collect membership fees upon applications.

- **High payout and proper payout ceiling.** There should be an existing data where average payouts could be based from. How much can you earn within a particular period? How much can you earn by volume and by hitting thresholds? How much commissions have the company already paid during their entire operation? You need to have an idea of your projected earning for every cumulative effort you will give.

Likewise, the payout ceiling should not be too low so as not to be an inconvenience should you be very successful with your marketing business. At the same time, it should not be too hard to hit, so you can withdraw easier and faster.

You also have to consider the terms of payment and methods used. A popular method is wiring through Paypal or directly to a bank account, but some still employ traditional payouts, like in the case of Google for its Adsense (not an affiliate program) where check is still the only option.

- **Reputation of the product and company.** It only needs common sense. Why would you join a marketing program with suspicious promises and rewards, or market products with questionable qualities and benefits? However, as simple as it might seem, there are still people who venture in affiliate programs and networking businesses without actually looking into reputation and credibility. They fall as victims to scams and illegitimate businesses in the end.

Promised rewards and commission rates are too tempting sometimes that people would no longer consider other factors but the earning potentials. However, projected incomes are mere figures in writing, and they do not necessarily translate to actual payouts if the company does not have the ability and resources to deliver their promises in the first place.

You need to look at the company's credibility amongst other marketers, such as affiliates, bloggers, networkers, etc. A simple online research will lead you to a lot of reviews and accounts of actual experiences. Ask around to safeguard your interest.

Also look at the company's operation if they have already been tested by time and unfortunate circumstances. You do not want to earn thousands of dollars in commission just to lose it before payout simply because the company has already gone out of business.

It also pays to check the reputation of the product, in particular, because there is a possibility that it already has impending negative image in the media or market. This is most especially true for food supplements and fitness equipment.

Some affiliate marketers do everything to promote certain types of food supplements for months just to discover that the latest scientific research about their products refute their effectiveness and safety. It happened to a lot of weight loss supplements before, where their potencies turned out to be nothing but mere marketing hypes.

- **Niche.** What is your line of specialization – your strengths and expertise? What are your interests that you think you can make you fulltime career? Narrow down your best picks and stick to a particular nature of interest; that will be your niche. Sticking with your niche is important because you have to establish authority and reputation in a specific field to become credible and reliable.

Creating a niche market is more important for marketers who sell ideas, contents and information, like in the case of bloggers, SEO marketers and article marketers. No one believes a know-it-all claim, so it will just be your own downfall to market everything there is under the sun without a clear path to take. By involving yourself in a line you are not familiar with, you are also taking the risk of losing interest in the end, rendering everything you built useless.

Do not jump to health and nutrition even if your line is automotives simply because an affiliate referred you to an affiliate program with high commission rate.

Choose your niche based on your actual knowledge and interest and not merely based on the opportunities awaiting you. As an affiliate, networking, multilevel, email, direct or social media marketer, you have to choose the product you are going to promote coming from your niche. Do not let every butterfly flying your direction get your attention. There will be a lot of opportunities in the marketing industry, but the real question will always be which one you can justify and commit to.

Chapter 2 – Finding What to Market

Now you know how to choose a product to market, but do you know how and where to find it? Finding is the hardest part because there are a lot of ideas everywhere and a lot of products to choose from. Of course, you can always do it the hard way of randomly researching different affiliate and networking sites on all possible sources, but that will eat up a lot of your time spent unwisely.

The best way to find the right product for you is by going directly to the sources. Consider this as the first part of your market research. Here are the best sources you can try.

Blogs and forums

Blogs and forums are reliable sources because people are talking about their actual experiences there, encouraging more discussions for other readers to see the pros and cons of each marketing program and product. These sites are open to refuting and confirmations, so their information are more credible than affiliate and networking sites that use marketing materials for contents. They are the perfect venues to cross-check for accuracy because they are updated, interactive and straightforward.

Go to blogs and forums sites then type "affiliate marketing," "network marketing," "MLM," "multilevel marketing," "home business," "online opportunity," or "income opportunity" in their search boxes, but you can also be specific by searching for the marketing program, product or company you are interested to join. It is certain that you have a lot of readings to do, but just be patient for your own sake.

Keyword research tools and analytics

These online tools are reliable aid for market research because they feed accurate and real-time information based on the actual movements of the market – the more than two billion people who go online everyday worldwide, who also spend more than $2.1 billion on affiliate marketing products alone. They analyze and crunch data according to actual search inputs of netizens in search engines. That means you identify specific trends and interests of your possible market segments that can also be narrowed down by locations. You will know what they want and what they are willing to spend for in advance.

News websites and peer-review journals

Look at trends and possible trends based on the latest scientific research and news, then, hype them up a bit by making these sources look like endorsements. Throw in some celebrity statements that you will interpret as endorsements, and you are up for a marketing homerun.

The medical and scientific communities are the most reliable sources of possible trends in the health and wellness industry. This encompasses the nutrition, fitness, food and beverage industries. Unfortunately, most of the time, scientific researches are preempted by manufacturing and processing companies that hype up inconclusive yet promising results. This is practically how manufacturers of dietary supplements get their clues and cues to penetrate larger markets and create more hype.

Researchers naturally look for potential treatments for various diseases, so they put to test dozens of natural chemical compounds, herbal plants and fruits, minerals and anything that might take medical science one step higher. Normally, a research takes years or even decades to complete, but businesses always find ways to create hype and earn money from it.

When scientists say that a fruit has a compound that can strengthen the immune system to fight cancer, businessmen can go around that and say the fruit can fight cancer. Technically speaking, it is not an illegal act since dietary supplements are labeled as "No Therapeutic Claim." Right there, a new lucrative product is born.

By looking at research journals, you can determine existing food supplements and other nutritional products that have high potential for business. Using article marketing, SEO marketing, attraction marketing, blogging and social media marketing, you can create demand when there is none.

News websites and magazines are also excellent media where you can find promising products because they are well-researched with insider information. You can bank on their resources by using their reports as your basis and support. Similarly, medical bulletins and shows also make for good sources. Ask Dr. Oz why he's always used as a source for marketing materials.

Direct Selling Association

Direct selling is not be mistaken for direct marketing, the former employing direct sellers dealing with and reaching customers vis-a-vis. However, if there is one group who knows a lot about direct marketing, affiliate marketing, network marketing and multilevel marketing, it would be the Direct Selling Association of America or the World Federation of Direct Selling Associations (WFDSA).

These organizations keep track of their member companies, so they know which ones make money and which ones have bigger potentials. Although these companies are classified as direct selling companies, they also use affiliate marketing, network marketing and MLM to expand their markets. As a matter of fact, networking is practically the principle behind their operations.

By looking at their top performers and member companies with unique and innovative products, you will get a bigger picture of the market trends and marketing trends. Most of them also accept affiliates and networkers, so you might just land on a good deal for your marketing career.

Online marketplace

These are sites that hold digital information products that are marketed by affiliates and those wanting to start a career in affiliate marketing. In the simplest sense, businesses that have products to sell hire marketers by placing their products under these online marketplaces, which does the hiring, promotion and compensation to all of its members.

The largest online marketplace today that you should check is Clickbank that holds a collection of more than 46,000 products for affiliate marketers to promote. It has attracted more than 1.5 million affiliates and has claimed to pay $2,000,000,000 in commissions in a single year alone. Clickbank has marketing presence in more than 200 countries, so your marketing career can expand across continents.

Other trustworthy online marketplaces to check out are Commission Junction, PayDotCom (spelled as is) and Linkshare.

Manufacturer's website

This is a basic way to become a marketer for businesses – by looking for products you want and think you can market, and going directly to their official websites to inquire for an affiliate or networking opportunity.

Many companies welcome registrations of marketers through their websites. Just look for the "Affiliate" section or button, then, register online. There might also be other variety of income opportunity that you can find.

For businesses that are not open to third party marketers just yet, you might want to inquire on the possibility of being their reseller instead. You won't get a certain percentage as commission, but you can resell products on prices of your own accord. This way, you will be marketing for the profit.

Online store

Amazon, Barnes and Noble and other online stores have their own bestselling lists – direct hints of what is marketable and what is not. These lists are more useful if you are registered as an affiliate of these sites.

For instance, Amazon has its own affiliate program in which interested individuals can register and be an affiliate with no commitment at all. Its affiliates simply need to promote products coming from its hundreds of thousands of available affiliate products with commissions starting from 4% to 20%, and close a successful sale. Amazon affiliates can ensure higher sales rate by promoting bestselling products that are already marketable and sellable by themselves. They offer bestselling lists for hundreds of categories, from kitchen faucets to computer tablets.

Even Yahoo! keeps track of bestselling items in certain categories. Whenever you have doubts about the marketability of your products, just verify them with bestselling lists. You can never go wrong with actual sales rank.

Review sites

Many review websites now hire their own affiliates because they also earn through referral fees. Naturally, products with better reviews have stronger market appeal. By sticking with well-received products, you are guaranteed with quality offerings that you will be proud to promote.

Many review sites also have rundown lists based on review scores. These are as reliable as bestselling lists or even better because you have more room to push further with your marketing tactics.

Chapter 3 – Jumpstarting Your Marketing Career

The next step to establishing a successful career in the marketing industry is starting the actual venture itself. This is the stage where you put all your plans and ideas into use by executing them through preparation and actual operation.

The biggest question at this point is how you will promote the products or services you have to market. Here are marketing strategies you can follow.

1. Set up a well-navigable website designed for SEO marketing

As a marketer, your website is your office, helpdesk, hotline, showroom, catalogue sales office, advertisement, billboard and practically everything you need to successfully fulfill your marketing tasks. Thus, it needs to be organized, clean, responsive, substantial and attractive.

A website has to be designed for function and not attraction because an attractive website is not necessarily functional and user-friendly while the latter is apt to be attractive. The internal navigation should be clear and easily accessible from the home page, feeding your readers with peeks of what your website is all about. The layout and design should also be controlled and reasonable.

The danger of designing your own website without sufficient knowledge is making it look like amateur, like a novice blogger trying to draw attention using uncoordinated colors, screaming animations and effects, impractical font styles and colors, inconsistent styles and themes and worse, misleading internal linking. Many bloggers usually use any designing feature they can add when creating a website. However, that does not really make their websites attractive but questionable.

Extravagant websites like an online carnival is seen by netizens as red flag because that is a practice commonly done by online scams. Have you ever noticed why "money-making" websites use screaming font sizes just to say you can be rich or make money within this and that period? Or display exaggerated testimonials complete with profiles and exact figures right at the home pages? These are websites designed for attraction and not function, and they are likely a scam, a scam you do not want to be identified with.

2. Choose the best domain name for your marketing venture

As a marketer, your domain is your business card and direct line. All your marketing efforts are practically centered in maximizing the capacity of your domain to attract new markets and reach out to your existing ones. Your email marketing, direct marketing, SEO marketing, blogging and social media marketing efforts practically end and goes back to your domain name – the location of your office that is your website. You might be surprised but many marketers only concentrate their efforts and attention on building the reputation of their domain names because at the end of the day, people will remember not your name but your domain name.

Some businesses buy already acquired domain names for as long as the addresses are guaranteed to bring in millions of visitors – and potential customers – back to their business sites and sales page. Similarly, many private individuals already buy domain names of businesses and trends that are likely to pick up and gain massive success in the future.

Attraction plays a very important role in rounding up your own market. Like on almost all businesses, their names are their most important attractions, and your own business name or brand should be clearly reflected in your domain name, or simply your website address. This is your face amongst millions of internet habitués – something that you will be remembered for even before they try out your product or service.

Although domain name does not compose everything that is to be considered for your search engine result page ranking, it will still count in your race to the top of search engines as algorithms first examine domain names in assessing the relevance of a site to a particular keyword/s that is being searched. It will also be your starting point in building your social media presence as your home pages and website should all be well-coordinated, both in name and content.

In choosing the best domain name for your marketing venture, you have to choose a name that best represents your product, service or content without sacrificing branding. Your domain name should clearly represent what you have to offer, dropping the hint at first glance, as much as possible. However, you have to be specific without sacrificing your brand.

A catering service located in Glendale can be easily found online with a domain name called *www.glendalecateringservices.com*. However, a very generic domain will ironically make you suffer obscurity, making you just another home business trying to make money but not offer a difference.

Usually, the product and service are already made obvious in the business name, which can also be the registered name or the trademark, like *Heaven Scent* for perfume business and *Bellisima Baby Bags* for, what else, but baby bags. The business name then becomes the domain name.

Mixing your own brand with a generic representation makes you standout and more memorable. It also makes it easier for you to find an available domain name that you can buy.

3. Generate marketing leads

Leads are the possible destinations of your messages, the receivers of your marketing efforts, and possibly, your customers. Once you already have the leads, starting your plans will be a lot easier. The hardest part, though, is getting your hands on that list.

You can collect your own marketing leads by keeping track of your analytics and checking out if some of them visit you under their social media accounts and blogs. You can approach them easier if you know what they are looking for in particular.

You can also leave a registration box in your site where interested visitors can leave their contact details, mostly emails, for your updates. Send them newsletters and activate feeds, so you can keep track of them and stay in touch. By creating threads in your comment sections, you can also identify specific people who are potentially your own followers.

There are existing market-databases that brokers sell to marketers. These brokers are marketers themselves who already collected marketing leads of their own through networks and years of marketing efforts. They sell these leads, but not all of them sell usable marketing leads for your own niche, of course. The Direct Selling Association of America has its own brokers who sell lists of possible customers together with their contact details to member companies and sales agents. You might want to have connection with an insider to have access to that.

Lastly, there are also software and online tools that generate marketing leads by collecting static information in the internet, producing you names, email addresses and phone numbers, while some sold tools already have existing market-databases. Usually, these software and tools scan other existing websites and blogs for contact details, then, feed the collected data to you. It is up to you how to use those contact details.

4. Maximize online forums

Forums are also a great tool in doing your market research because of the volume of customer feedbacks you can get from them. You go at the center of their discussions to determine the key issues customers want to be addressed. Some of your most reliable marketing leads can also come from these threads because you can already analyze the reception of your market through interaction.

By stirring interest through discussions, you can also establish yourself as an expert that is credible, reliable and knowledgeable of what people are looking for and interest in. Offer your service by giving advice and helping others. This is a fast way to redirect curious parties straight to your website. By establishing yourself amongst a circle of people with similar interests, you also make it easier to penetrate their consciousness and sell without them knowing.

It is easier to influence your market when you already gained their trust and loyalty, and that is only possible by letting them think that you are beneficial to them in any way possible.

Conclusion

Thank you again for purchasing this book!

I hope this book was able to help you to start your marketing career the best way possible.

The next step is to start following the tips given here and practicing them with utmost commitment.

Finally, if you enjoyed this book, please take the time to share your thoughts and post a review on Amazon. We do our best to reach out to readers and provide the best value we can. Your positive review will help us achieve that. It'd be greatly appreciated!

Thank you and good luck!

Book 2:

Money Management Makeover

BY J.J. JONES

The Ultimate Plan for Financial Success with Managing Your Money by Budgeting and Saving!

Table Of Contents

Introduction

I want to thank you and congratulate you for purchasing the book, *"Money Management Makeover - The Ultimate Plan for Financial Success with Managing Your Money by Budgeting and Saving"*.

This book contains proven steps and strategies on how to assess your current financial situation and make sound plans in order to get rid of debt, start an emergency fund, and achieve your financial goals. This book will help you get started on budgeting, saving and investing your money to gain financial wealth and freedom.

Thanks again for purchasing this book, I hope you enjoy it!

Chapter 1 - Assess Your Current Financial Situation

If you want to become financially stable but don't know where to begin, then you should start by first determining your exact financial health status. You need to be able to identify how much money you have, how much you owe, and how much you need to have. Knowing these facts will help you create changes to improve your finances and achieve your goals.

Step 1: Create Financial Statements

There are two types of financial statements that you will need, and these are cash flow statement and net worth statement.

Cash-Flow Statement. This information is a comparison between your monthly net income and your average monthly expenses. You begin creating your cash flow statement by listing down all of your monthly expenses and then adding up the total amount of monthly expenses. After that, you list down all of your monthly net income (deductions not included) and add them all up as well. Deduct the total amount of monthly expenses from the total amount of your income. The difference defines your current cash flow.

Your current cash flow can help you determine what changes need to be made in order to increase the amount. This will entail you to create a budget, increase your income, and minimize your expenses if your goal is to save more money.

The following are common income sources: salary, earnings from part-time jobs, child support and alimony

Common monthly expenses are: rent or mortgage, food and groceries, utilities, medical expenses, property taxes, home maintenance costs, insurance, savings and investment contributions, credit cards, child care and child support, clothing, loans, memberships, transportation, and leisure.

Net Worth Statement. Your net worth is your total assets in comparison to your total liabilities. Assets are your cash, property and other valuable items. Your liabilities are the money that you owe.

Assets are in the form of: cash (including the amount in your checking and savings accounts), collectibles, Certificates of Deposits or CODs, Money Market Funds, Life insurance cash value, real estate market value, business property or assets, personal valuables (such as gold and silver), and retirement accounts.

Liabilities are: bills, credit card balances, loan balances, mortgage balances, taxes owed and home-equity credit lines.

Step 2: Organize and Review Your Financial Records

Create a filing system (both soft and hard copies) of your financial records to keep in track. Form a habit of regularly updating it. You should also include your partner or spouse's financial records.

The files to be included are all of your bank, loan, credit card and investment accounts, your legal documents including insurance policies, real estate titles and tax files, your billing statements and correspondents, and other important documents such as your Social Security retirement and other benefits.

After you have successfully organized all of your financial records, you can start reviewing them to help you pinpoint where you are losing money and where you can save money. This includes knowing your current credit status and how to fix any problems that you might have. Also, determine how much you currently can afford in case of a financial crisis.

Now that you have a clear view of your current financial situation, you can move on to creating a financial plan as well as a solid budget.

Chapter 2 - Create a Financial Plan

A solid financial plan should be organized and written down. It is your guide to achieving your financial goals each step of the way. It also serves as a reminder of your financial responsibilities towards yourself and your future.

Steps in Creating a Financial Plan

Step 1: Set your financial goals

Think about what you really want to achieve in short-term and long-term. These might include further education for yourself or college education for your children, plans in getting a promotion or setting up your own business, buying a new house or moving to a new place, and the lifestyle that you wish to maintain after you retire. You can also include leisure goals such as going on a vacation.

Step 2: Make an estimate of your projected income

Most likely one of your financial goals is to increase your income. You can distinguish the different sources of income based on five major categories: career, business, investments, inheritance and unexpected income. Keep in mind that it is always best to have more than one income source.

Career income is when you are the one who is employed and received fixed salary.

Business income is when you profit from running your own business or from products or services that you generate.

Investments are your stocks, bonds, money market funds, real estate and CODs.

Inheritance is money coming from other people.

Unexpected income is money coming from bonuses, gifts, lottery winnings and other similar sources. You should already have a financial plan ready for when you do receive unexpected income so that you will not end up spending it away, and instead help make it grow even bigger.

Step 3: Create a timeline for your goals

With each financial goal that you have, come up with concrete steps on how to achieve them. You should also create "deadlines" for each of these steps so that you will be reminded of what to do each day in order to bring you closer to your goals.

Your goals should be divided into four main categories: immediate future (within 12 months), near future (5 year span), extended future (10 year span), and distant future (after ten years).

Step 4: Develop an income strategy that will help you achieve your goals based on your timeline. You will also need a solid budget and an expenses and allotment tracker to prevent yourself from overspending on unnecessary expenses.

Step 5: Come up with a way to fully commit yourself to your financial plan. A lot of people create very good financial plans but do not follow them, mainly because they become swayed into spending on things that they do not need and throwing themselves off track.

Chapter 3 - Create a Budget Plan and Stick to It

A budget is technically the amount of money that you allocate for specific purposes, particularly your basic needs. Most people make the mistake of treating their budget as a "suggestion" instead of a rule, which is why their liabilities constantly increase and their net worth decreases.

The tool to increasing your wealth is your income, and the best way to handle your income power is with a monthly budget. Not having a budget is like letting water flow carelessly in all directions, and before you know it you will have ended up with nothing. The budgets are the channels that control the flow of water. You decide how big the channels are, where they are heading.

The Habit of Creating a Monthly Budget

You have made a wise decision to plan how you will be spending your money. Creating a budget is a habit. In fact, you will need to create a new budget for the next month at the end of the current month. After all, each month presents different agendas, from holidays, birthdays, insurance bills, and whatnot. It is difficult - if not impossible - to stick to a single budget plan all of the time. Plan to create a new monthly budget a day or two before the start of each month so that you can treat each month as a fresh start.

Practice the Zero-based Budget Strategy

Zero-based budget is to make sure that the difference between your income and the outgo is zero. If you have paid for all the expenses and you have some money left (say, 300 dollars) you are not finished with your budget yet. You must be able to tell where it will go - such as paying off your debts, putting it in your emergency fund or investing it - or else you will spend it on a liability purchase.

Statistics show that those who follow a zero-based budget were able to pay off 19 percent more of their debt and save 18 percent more of their money compared to those who do not follow it.

Avoid Wasteful Money Burners

If your expenses far outweigh your income, then you will need to get rid of some spending habits. Even if you do increase your income substantially you will still end up spending a lot more if you stick to old, overspending habits.

For instance, impulse shopping is one major money burning habit. If it's not in your list of needs, do not purchase it no matter how "great" the deal is. You will figure out a way to buy it in the future when you do need it.

You shell out hundreds of dollars more each month from eating out. This monetary value is higher compared to the time you have "saved" from preparing your own meals. Learn how to plan your meals ahead and shop for cheap but healthy ingredients.

Determine How Much You Need to Spend Each Month

Review your list of expenses and highlight the ones that you cannot avoid spending on, such as your rent or mortgage, insurance, transportation to and from work, utility bills, and groceries and so on. Total the amount and deduct it from your total monthly income. It would be even better if you figured out ways to lower this number as well.

For instance, you can anticipate sales, collect coupons and buy generic brands in order to minimize grocery expenses and put what you have saved into paying off your debts and eventually into your emergency fund and investments.

Think of clever ways for you and your family to stay entertained without using up too much electricity or spending on trips and such.

Learn to swap items with friends and neighbours instead of always buying to avoid additional purchases, such as clothes and tools.

After you have determined the expenses for your needs, divide the remaining amount between saving up for your emergency fund, paying off debt and your wants. The rule of thumb is to set aside 60 percent for expenses for your needs, 20 percent to pay off debt (and eventually to put into your emergency fund and investments), and 20 percent for your wants.

The 5 Basic Steps of a Budget Plan

There are 5 basic steps in a budget plan. Each step will require you to make several changes in your current lifestyle. It depends on how much change you can tolerate, but the sooner you increase your allotment for savings and investments the sooner you will gain financial wealth.

Step 1: Create a starter emergency fund

It is very important to have some money set aside for emergencies. The recommended amount is 1,000 dollars to cover minor emergencies. However, you need to start building this immediately so that you can pay off your debts as soon as possible.

A good suggestion in increasing the amount of money allotted to your starter emergency fund is to try to save around 10 percent of your budget and put it into your starter. This is in addition to the 20 percent that you set aside for it. For example, if your budget for your groceries is 500 dollars, figure out a way to lower it to 450 dollars so that you can put the 50 dollars into your starter.

Step 2: Pay off all of your debts

In chapter 4 you will learn how to get rid of debt. It is very important to get rid of your debts as soon as possible otherwise the interest will just compound and you will end up paying for much, much more than the value of the items that you paid for on credit.

For example, if you bought a towel with your credit card for 20 dollars, the cost of your 20 dollar quality budget will turn into 60 dollars within a few months' time if you do not pay off your credit card debts right now.

Step 3: Fully fund your emergency fund

After you have paid off all of your debts, you can now move on to building an emergency fund. This will be discussed in detail in Chapter 5.

Step 4: Start investing for retirement

It is inevitable that we will all age and not be as able-bodied as we used to, that is why we need to save up for this part of our lives. After you have fully funded your emergency fund, you will need to start setting aside some money for a long-term investment in order to reap the rewards 10 to 40 years from now.

Step 5: Start investing for your personal financial goals

Your budget should accommodate the money that you would like to set aside for your personal financial goals. Review your financial plan and your timeframe so that you can plan your budget around these goals.

Budgeting Habits to Make

Budgeting is not about depriving yourself. It is about being careful with where your money is going, so that you do not end up getting robbed of a financially stable future. Develop these sound spending and budgeting habits to help make things go smoothly for you:

Monitor and analyze your spending regularly.

It is important to start the habit of taking note of your expenses in a personal ledger and to compare it with how much your overall income is. It might sound tedious but it actually won't take more than 5 minutes of your time. By tracking what you spend every day, you will be able to identify unnecessary expenditures and avoid them in the future. Remember, a small hole can sink a big ship.

Determine how much more you will be able to save every month.

Instead of thinking about how to spend your money, it is best to start thinking about how you are going to be able to save more money. Even better if you start thinking how to earn even more money. Be creative and frugal in spending for your needs and wants. For example, learn to negotiate in order to get discounts and freebies, and look for cheaper places where you can regularly buy your groceries and such. Even small savings will add up if you look at the big picture.

Do not put all of your cash in the same wallet.

Even some of the most financially sound individuals find it very difficult not to be tempted to spend their money on something. If you know that you tend to make impulse buys, you will be able to avoid it by not bringing all of your cash with you wherever you go. Also, if you are going someplace without meaning to buy anything (such as going out for coffee with friends), bring only enough cash that you have set as your budget and leave your credit cards behind.

Save first before spending.

Most people still have the old habit of spending first before and then save up what is left, if any. Whenever acquire income, make it a habit to head straight to the bank and make a deposit into your savings first before you buy anything. This will help keep things in perspective, because sometimes people become overwhelmed with their income and start to think of how they will spend this much money when in fact the remaining amount for their wants is minimal compared to how much they should save to achieve their financial goals.

Chapter 4 - Get Rid of Debt ASAP

The key to getting out of debt is to start paying off the smallest first in order to start a momentum. This might sound contrary to the common notion that you should start paying off the debt with the highest interest but it is actually highly effective. It is called the Snowball Method and it has much to do with human behaviour.

When you start paying off your smaller debts first, you become motivated to move on to the bigger ones after you have crossed them off of your list. After you have accumulated 1,000 dollars in a passbook or checking account for your starter emergency fund, concentrate and make an effort to pay off all of your debt as soon as possible (except the mortgage).

Step 1: List Down Your Debts

The first step is to make a list of all of your debts, starting with the smallest balance. Do not think about the interest rates or terms, but if there are two debts with the same payoffs, you can put the one with the higher interest rate before the other one on the list.

Step 2: Focus on the Deadline

Using your cash flow statements and budget, create a timeline on how you can pay off your debt quickly. Keep tracking how much you have paid off to build momentum on your goal to financial freedom.

Step 3: Focus on the Smallest Debt First

Concentrate all of your effort and resources to pay off the smallest debt while continuing to pay for the minimum payments of the others. Once you have completely paid off the smallest, move on to the next one down the list and do the same.

Alternative Methods to Pay Off Debt

The Snowball method is applicable for most people, but if you know for sure that you are financially disciplined you can choose to pay off your credit card debts and loans with the higher interest first in order to further minimize costs and get rid of debt even faster.

Those who cannot afford to pay all of the minimum requirements while paying off the smallest debt at the same time can also choose to pay off the debts with the higher interest rates to keep them from compounding.

Handling Consumer Debt

Do not get into deeper debt while you are paying off your debt otherwise you will be trapped in a vicious cycle. This means you should cancel all of your credit cards and keep a Visa or MasterCard debit card instead. However, if you are to apply the strategy below, you must not cancel the high-interest rate credit cards first or else your credit score will go down. Just make sure to stop using the card with the higher interest rate.

One strategy that you can apply to help lower your credit card debt interest rate is to apply for a lower-rate credit card. You will need to have a really good credit report and score to obtain this, and your debt outstanding should not have too big of a difference compared to your income. Once approved, you can transfer the outstanding balance from your higher interest rate credit cards to the lower one and start paying them off obsessively.

Another option is to negotiate for a better deal from the current credit card company. Call the bank and tell them that you want to cancel your card because you want to choose a competitor that does not have an annual fee and has a lower interest rate. Chances are the bank will match the terms of this competitor; otherwise you can go ahead and apply for the lower interest rate card before cancelling.

If you are facing extreme debt, you will need to take action immediately. This can be overwhelming so choose to seek help from a credit counselling agency. Do plenty of research on the company before getting them as some of them are funded by the feeds paid by creditors.

Ask them if they offer debt management programs, and if they do you should avoid them. A debt management program is when you are on a repayment plan with your creditors but the agency is paid a monthly fee for handling the payments. Get a specific price quote and get a contract in writing. Avoid agencies with a high upfront fee. If the agency advises that you stop paying your bills, avoid them as well as they might just take your money and disappear. Lastly ask for their license and the qualifications of their counsellors, and assurance of confidentiality and security.

Chapter 5 - Safeguard Yourself and Your Money

Once you have paid off all of your debts, you can breathe a big sigh of relief and give yourself a pat on the back for a job well done. Now you have a clean slate and move on to building your financial wealth.

Readiness and protection are very important when it comes to financial stability, this is why you will need to create an emergency fund and review your insurance plans.

Fill up your Emergency Fund

You can now concentrate on fully funding your emergency fund. Your emergency fund will help you survive through sudden financial problems such as unemployment or hospitalization. It should be enough to cover for your expenses for 3 to 6 months. Place your emergency fund in a passbook account to prevent you from touching it or spending it on less important things.

Focus on building your emergency fund up to 3 months first, and after that you can split 50 percent on funding the last 3 months and the other 50 percent on investments.

Get Insured

Minor emergencies can be covered by an emergency fund, but major ones such as calamities, illness and legal disputes can really drain your finances. The best way to protect you and your money would be to get the right insurance policy.

The ones you need the most are health insurance, disability insurance and life insurance if you have dependents.

Health Insurance Tips.

Find a good health insurance policy that has a high deductible. This is the amount of medical claims that you need to pay out first using your emergency funds before the insurance coverage pays you for it. You should also look for one with the highest co-payment. This is the amount that you need to shell out when service is rendered. A quality health insurance should have major medical coverage including laboratory work, ancillary charges and hospital care.

Disability Insurance Tips.

A disability insurance will protect your income for you, especially when you become disabled and cannot work anymore. If you are employed and have long-term disability coverage, ask the benefits department of the company that you are working for on the details of the policy and check whether it will pay benefits when you reach a certain age.

Life Insurance Tips.

If you have dependents, you will want to protect them from becoming financially burdened in case something happens to you. But if you are single, independent and do not have any children then you do not need one. It is recommended that you purchase a low cost term insurance instead of cash value insurance, because you will want to invest separately.

Chapter 6 - Put Your Money in Investments

Saving your money in a bank account alone will not help you in the long run because of inflation. The interest rates of a typical savings account are a lot less compared to inflation. Investing your hard earned money is therefore the wisest choice to make especially if you want to beat inflation. Investing takes a lot of research and discipline, but the efforts are really worth it.

There are two major ways to invest your money, the first is to lend it and gain income from interest rates and the second is to buy assets.

Lending Investments

Lending investments are in the form of bonds, treasury bills, and certificates of deposit or COD. You become a lender when you lend your money to a bank the federal government or any other organization that offers this setup. The goal is for you to get paid the interest in addition to the original investment that you have lent. There is no assurance as to whether you will indeed reap what you sow, that is why you must do plenty of research first.

Ownership Investments

The three best choices to boost your financial wealth are to invest in ownership investments, which are stocks, real estate, and small business.

Stocks are the shares of ownership that are in a company, and the most common ownership investment vehicle. You become an owner once you put your money in as an asset on real estate or a company that will generate profits. As a stockholder you get a share in the profits called dividends, which are paid quarterly to shareholders. If the company's business goes well, you gain too. Vice versa, if the business does not succeed. Do not invest in individual stocks if you do not know everything about it. Keep in mind that researching on it can become a full time job and will take up a lot of your time and some money.

If you are new to investing and would like to invest in a low-cost investment plan, research on mutual funds and exchange-traded funds or ETFs instead. Mutual funds are a collection of funds from many investors like you and the capital is invested to produce gain. ETFs are a lot like mutual funds, except they trade on a major stock exchange.

Becoming a real estate owner or investor is a financially rewarding type of ownership investment. Land is a commodity that generally steadily increases in value over time, making it a safe investment as long as you have done your research. For example, buying your own home is a good way to begin investing in real estate. The equity that will build over time will really improve your net worth.

The last ownership investment is to go into small business. You can either start your own small business or you can invest in others' small businesses and gain profit along with them. Many people have successfully achieved financial wealth while running a business. Naturally, it requires complete dedication, focus and really good ideas for it to work.

The best advice when it comes to investment is to spread the risk through diversification. It adheres to the old saying, "don't put all of your eggs in the same basket." In order to lower your risk of losing everything, allot your investment capital in different types of investments such as real estate, bonds, stocks and small businesses. You should also diversify them in both domestic and international markets. This is called asset allocation. In the long run, your decisions in asset allocation will determine the total return for your diversified portfolio.

Know how your level of risk tolerance and consider other factors in mind, such as your financial goals as well as your age. The younger you are, the more risks you will be able to cope with.

Conclusion

Thank you again for purchasing this book!

I hope this book was able to help you to plan your financial goals carefully and fully understand your current financial health.

The next step is to take action and work on achieving your financial goals. Work hard and make your money work for you as well. With discipline, determination and focus you will definitely gain the financial freedom that you deserve.

Finally, if you enjoyed this book, please take the time to share your thoughts and post a review on Amazon. We do our best to reach out to readers and provide the best value we can. Your positive review will help us achieve that. It'd be greatly appreciated!

Thank you and good luck!

Check Out My Other Books

Below you'll find some of my other popular books that are popular on Amazon and Kindle as well. Simply click on the links below to check them out. Alternatively, you can visit my author page on Amazon to see other work done by me.

Marketing Money Mastery

http://amzn.to/1hxUaj6

"Debt Free Forever"

http://amzn.to/1qrgldh

Money Management Makeover

http://amzn.to/1hAU8Z7

Single Women and Budgets

http://amzn.to/WPRJ3M